Driving
Standards
Agency

GW00771249

The **OFFICIAL DSA GUIDE** to
TRACTOR
and SPECIALIST VEHICLE
Driving Tests

2012/2013

SURREY LIBRARIES

REF

London: TSO

Written and compiled by the Learning Materials department of the Driving Standards Agency (DSA).

© Crown copyright 2012

All rights reserved.

No part of this publication may be reproduced in any material form without the written permission of the copyright owner except in accordance with the provisions of the Copyright, Designs and Patents Act 1988 or under the terms of a licence issued by the Copyright Licensing Agency Ltd. Crown copyright material is reproduced with permission of the Controller of HMSO and the Queen's Printer for Scotland.

First edition Crown copyright 1999
Second edition Crown copyright 2001
Third edition Crown copyright 2012

ISBN 978 0 11553252 8

A CIP catalogue record for this book is available from the British Library

Other titles in the Driving Skills series

The Official DSA Guide to Driving – the essential skills
The Official DSA Theory Test for Car Drivers
The Official DSA Theory Test for Car Drivers (DVD-ROM)
The Official DSA Guide to Learning to Drive
Prepare for your Practical Driving Test (DVD)
DSA Driving Theory Quiz (DVD)
The Official Highway Code Interactive CD-ROM

The Official DSA Theory Test iPhone App
The Official DSA Theory Test Kit iPhone App
The Official Highway Code iPhone App

The Official DSA Guide to Riding – the essential skills
The Official DSA Theory Test for Motorcyclists
The Official DSA Theory Test for Motorcyclists (DVD-ROM)
The Official DSA Guide to Learning to Ride
Better Biking – the official DSA training aid (DVD)

The Official DSA Guide to Driving Buses and Coaches
The Official DSA Guide to Driving Goods Vehicles
The Official DSA Theory Test for Drivers of Large Vehicles
The Official DSA Theory Test for Drivers of Large Vehicles (DVD-ROM)
Driver CPC – the official DSA guide for professional bus and coach drivers
Driver CPC – the official DSA guide for professional goods vehicle drivers

The Official DSA Guide to Hazard Perception (DVD)

Every effort has been made to ensure that the information contained in this publication is accurate at the time of going to press. The Stationery Office cannot be held responsible for any inaccuracies. Information in this book is for guidance only.

All metric and imperial conversions in this book are approximate.

Acknowledgements

The Driving Standards Agency (DSA) would like to thank the staff of the following organisations for their contribution to the production of this publication:

Chris Tallis Farm Machinery Ltd, Evesham
Cotswold Roller Hire, Evesham
Ravenhill Farm Services, Hereford
Specialist Vehicle Training, Norwich

We're turning over a new leaf.

RECYCLED
Paper made from recycled material
FSC® C002151
www.fsc.org

Find us online

⊘ GOV.UK - Simpler, clearer, faster

GOV.UK is the best place to find government services and information for

- car drivers
- motorcyclists
- driving licences
- driving and riding tests
- towing a caravan or trailer
- medical rules
- driving and riding for a living
- online services.

Visit **www.gov.uk and try it out!**

You can also find contact details for DSA and other motoring agencies like DVLA at **www.gov.uk**

You'll notice that links to **GOV.UK**, the UK's new central government site, don't always take you to a specific page. This is because this new kind of site constantly adapts to what people really search for and so such static links would quickly go out of date. Try it out. Simply search what you need from your preferred search site or from **www.gov.uk** and you should find what you're looking for. You can give feedback to the Government Digital Service from the website.

Driving Standards Agency

The Driving Standards Agency (DSA) is an executive agency of the Department for Transport. You'll see its logo at theory and practical test centres.

DSA aims to promote road safety through the advancement of driving standards, by

- establishing and developing high standards and best practice in driving and riding on the road; before people start to drive, as they learn, and after they pass their test
- ensuring high standards of instruction for different types of driver and rider
- conducting the statutory theory and practical tests efficiently, fairly and consistently across the country
- providing a centre of excellence for driver training and driving standards
- developing a range of publications and publicity material designed to promote safe driving for life.

The Driving Standards Agency recognises and values its customers. It will treat all its customers with respect, and deliver its services in an objective, polite and fair way.

The Driver and Vehicle Agency (DVA) is an executive agency within the Department of the Environment for Northern Ireland.

Its primary aim is to promote and improve road safety through the advancement of driving standards and implementation of the government's policies for improving the mechanical standards of vehicles.

dvani.gov.uk

www.gov.uk/dsa

Contents

section **one**
GETTING STARTED

This section covers

- Your driving licence
- Vehicle types
- Other documents
- Learning to drive
- Study materials
- The practical driving test
- Booking your test
- Attending your practical test

A message from the chief driving examiner

You may be planning to drive a tractor or other specialist vehicle occasionally, or you may do so regularly as part of your job.

This book is for the driver who needs to take a driving test using a specialist or unusual vehicle. These include agricultural tractors (category F), road rollers (category G), track-laying vehicles (category H) and mowing machines or pedestrian-controlled vehicles (category K).

The purpose of the test is to assess basic road safety procedures. It's vitally important to develop the correct attitude towards driving – showing responsibility and consideration to other road users. Only those who can do this will earn the right to drive without L plates (or D plates in Wales).

The preparation you make and the training you receive before the test are the foundation for gaining further skills and experience. It's important that you understand the principles of what you've learned and put them into practice. By passing your test you'll have shown that you can drive safely, but the test is just one stage in your driving career. You shouldn't assume that if you pass your test you're a good driver with nothing more to learn.

During your practical test your examiner will want to see you driving to the standards explained in this book. Those standards are given here in an easy-to-read style with illustrations and guidance for these specialist vehicles. However, driving is never predictable. Road conditions or circumstances, coupled with the unusual characteristics of these vehicles, will demand that you're able to assess any situation and apply the guidance given in this book.

Make sure that your aim is 'safe driving for life'.

Lesley Young

Chief Driving Examiner

Your driving licence

For the category of vehicle you intend to drive you **MUST** have either

- a signed, valid GB or Northern Ireland provisional driving licence

  or

- a signed, valid, full driving licence.

Driving licences are issued by the Driver and Vehicle Licensing Agency (DVLA). Application form D1 can be requested online from **www.gov.uk** or obtained from any post office. In Northern Ireland the issuing authority is the Driver and Vehicle Agency (DVA) and the form is a DL1. For more information, see **nidirect.gov.uk/ applying-for-a-provisional-driving-licence**

When you receive any licence from DVLA (or DVA in NI), you should

- check all the details to make sure they're correct. If you need to contact DVLA, the telephone number is 0300 790 6801 (DVA is 0845 402 4000)
- keep it in a safe place.

Vehicle types

Category F – agricultural or forestry tractors

Agricultural or forestry tractors

- have two or more axles
- are constructed for use as tractors for work off the road in connection with agriculture or forestry.

There are many types of agricultural vehicles in this category. If you have any doubt you should check with DVLA; the telephone number is 0300 790 6801 (DVA is 0845 402 4000).

Age limit To drive these tractors on public roads you must be at least 16 years old. At 16 years old

- you're restricted to tractors no more than 2.45 metres wide
- you can drive on the road only when travelling to, from and during a driving test until you've passed your category F driving test.

At 17 years old you can

- drive any agricultural tractor
- drive unaccompanied on the road while displaying red L plates (D plates in Wales).

Speed limit Agricultural tractors have a speed restriction of

- 20 mph (32 km/h) unless the vehicle and/or any attachments are over 3.5 metres in width, when the limit is reduced to 12 mph (18 km/h)
- 40 mph (64 km/h) if the vehicle meets construction and use regulations, including the fitment of
  - safety glass
  - horns
  - additional lights
  - speedometer
  - wing mirrors
  - additional noise suppression
  - brakes up to goods vehicle braking standards.

Number plates An agricultural machine **MUST** have a vertical number plate displayed either

- on the rear of the vehicle

or

- on both sides of the vehicle.

Category G – road rollers

G

Before you apply for a provisional licence to drive a vehicle in category G, you must have passed a test for a vehicle in category B.

Age limits At 17 years old there are two types of road roller you can drive. These include road rollers that aren't steam-propelled but

* have metal rollers
* weigh less than 11.69 tonnes unladen.

At 21 years old you can drive other road rollers. These include road rollers that

* have pneumatic, resilient or elastic tyres
* weigh more than 11.69 tonnes unladen
* are steam-propelled.

Speed limits Road rollers with resilient tyres are limited to a maximum speed of 20 mph (32 km/h). Road rollers with metal rollers are limited to 5 mph (approx 8 km/h).

Category H – track-laying vehicles steered by their tracks

Before you can apply for a provisional licence to drive a vehicle in category H you must have passed a test for a vehicle in category B.

Age limit Generally, you must be at least 21 years old to drive these vehicles, although you may be able to drive them at 17 if you're a member of the armed forces or if the maximum authorised mass of the vehicle isn't more than 3500 kg.

Speed limits Vehicles with sprung suspension and 'resilient' material between the rims of their weight-carrying rollers and the road surface (this could be rubber or other resilient material fitted as blocks on the tracks or resilient tracks) are limited to 20 mph (32 km/h). Vehicles not so fitted are limited to 5 mph (8 km/h).

Category K – mowing machines or pedestrian-controlled vehicles

Mowing machines are specialist ride-on grass-cutting vehicles with permanent grass-cutting equipment.

Age limit You must be at least 16 years old to drive these vehicles.

A pedestrian-controlled vehicle is a powered vehicle where the operator walks with the vehicle, and doesn't ride on it. (Pedestrian-controlled mowing machines aren't treated as motor vehicles and so don't need a driving licence.)

Age limit You must be at least 16 years old to operate these vehicles.

Other documents

Vehicle excise duty

Vehicle excise duty (VED) is often called road tax.

The owners or the operators of all mechanically propelled vehicles must display the required vehicle excise licence (tax disc) on the vehicle. A tax disc **MUST NOT** be transferred from one vehicle to another.

The registered keeper is responsible for taxing a vehicle or making a Statutory Off-Road Notification (SORN). The keeper must inform DVLA (DVA in NI) when the vehicle is off the road, has been sold, scrapped or exported, otherwise they remain liable for taxing it.

If you don't relicense your vehicle (or declare SORN), you'll automatically incur a penalty. DVLA (DVA in NI) carries out a computer check each month to identify those vehicles without a valid tax disc.

Applying To ensure your tax disc is up to date, fill in

- the relevant section of the renewal reminder form V11, or
- form V10 which is available from post offices.

In both cases, take the completed form to a licence-issuing post office to obtain your tax disc. Alternatively, you can apply online at **www.gov.uk**
Tel 0300 123 4321
Minicom 0300 790 6201.

Statutory Off-Road Notification

(SORN) If you don't intend to use or keep the vehicle on a public road, you can declare SORN so that you don't have to pay road tax. You can declare SORN by

- filling in the relevant section of your renewal reminder form V11 and taking it to a post office
- filling in a SORN declaration form V890 (available from post offices or downloadable from **www.gov.uk** and sending it to DVLA (DVA in NI))
- making a declaration on 'application for refund' forms V14 and V33 if you're also applying for a refund and the vehicle is to remain in your possession.

Alternatively, you can apply online at **www.gov.uk**
Tel 0300 123 4321
Minicom 0300 790 6201.

Duty payable The rate of vehicle excise duty payable is dependent on the vehicle's

- category
- construction and use
- age.

Contact your local licence-issuing post office or vehicle registration office for the current rates of vehicle excise licence duty. You can pay it either yearly or half-yearly. A table ('rates of vehicle tax') showing tax rates for various vehicles (Form V149) can be downloaded from **www.gov.uk**

Exemptions All vehicles, except buses and goods vehicles used commercially, are exempt from VED if they were constructed before 1 January 1973.

Additionally, the following vehicles are exempt from payment of VED

- certain tractors
- vehicles designed solely for agricultural use (combine harvesters, sprayers, etc)
- mowing machines
- snow ploughs
- gritting machines
- electrical vehicles
- steam vehicles.

All exempted vehicles will continue to need registration and will need to be licensed annually. You'll need to produce an appropriate MOT certificate (if applicable) and certificate of insurance in order to obtain a nil tax disc for display on the vehicle.

Insurance

Driving without insurance is

- illegal
- irresponsible.

Should you cause injury to anyone or damage to property, it could be expensive and result in criminal prosecution. Before you take the vehicle on the public road, make sure you have proper insurance cover.

Third-party cover This is the legal minimum cover. The 'third party' is any person you might injure or whose property you might damage. You're not covered for damage to your vehicle or injury to yourself.

Third party, fire and theft insurance
The same as third-party cover, except that it also covers against your vehicle being stolen or damaged by fire.

Comprehensive insurance This is the best type of cover, but the most expensive. As well as covering other persons and property from injury and damage, it also covers damage to your vehicle.

What's insured This varies from company to company. Read the small print and ask the insurer or broker if you're in any doubt.

Insurance companies often don't pay the first £50 or £100 of any claim – this is called the 'excess'.

The certificate of insurance A short and simple document which certifies

- who's insured
- the vehicle(s) covered
- the kind of cover
- the period of cover
- the main conditions.

You'll have to produce the certificate

- if the police ask you
- when renewing the vehicle excise licence
- if you're involved in an incident.

The policy document This contains the full details of the insurance contract.

This is known as the 'small print', and usually it's written in legal language – although some companies have simplified their policies.

If there's anything you don't understand, ask your broker or the insurance company to explain it.

> **Remember,** you MUST have insurance to use your vehicle on the road.

Road traffic incidents

You **MUST** stop if you're involved in an incident where

- any person is injured
- any vehicle or property, apart from your own, is damaged
- certain animals not in your vehicle, including large farm animals and dogs, are injured.

Give to anyone having reasonable cause to ask for them

- your name and address
- the vehicle owner's name and address if different
- the registration number of the vehicle
- the vehicle make and model
- the name and address of your insurance company
- details of your insurance certificate.

You **MUST** report the incident to the police, in person, as soon as practicable and in any event within 24 hours. (In NI you **MUST** report the incident immediately.) If there has been an injury, you must also give insurance details to the police.

If you can't produce the insurance documents when you report the incident, you must do so within seven days at a police station of your choice.

14

Learning to drive

An approved driving instructor (ADI) (car) is approved by DSA to teach learner drivers for payment.

To help you practise, you should find someone who

- is an experienced driver of the type of vehicle you wish to drive
- can explain clearly and simply the skills you must learn
- is patient and tactful
- builds your confidence.

If your employer needs you to take a test in a specialist vehicle, suitable instruction may be arranged for you.

Practice

When you practise on public roads your vehicle must display red L plates to the front and rear (in Wales, you can use D plates if you prefer).

Your practice vehicle must be properly insured for you to drive. It can be useful if your instructor is also insured, so that they can give you a practical demonstration of the skills you need to learn.

Always make sure your vehicle is roadworthy before using it on the road.

To practise driving a tractor on the road you must be at least 17 years old. If you're 16, you can drive a tractor on the road only

- when driving to or returning from your driving test appointment
- when you've passed your driving test.

Where and how to practise When you're first learning to control your vehicle it's important that you start somewhere quiet with lots of space. Try to find somewhere with

- no pedestrians
- no obstructions
- no moving vehicles
- a good flat surface.

You should also make sure that you have the landowner's permission.

Few, if any, specialist vehicles are fitted with dual controls, or even have space for two people on board. Your instructor

- may have to walk alongside you calling out advice
- will need to keep out of your way but be close enough to see what you're doing.

Learn and practise each basic skill before moving on to more complicated techniques. Time spent learning the basics properly will never be wasted.

When you're on the road, follow the advice in The Highway Code. Always drive on the road unless you're working with your vehicle on a pavement or a grass verge.

Category K vehicles may be restricted in performance and not as easy to see as other vehicles. Make yourself as noticeable as possible by wearing some form of visibility aid such as a high-visibility waistcoat, vest or jacket.

Are you ready?

Listen to your instructor and follow their advice about when to take your test.

Make sure that you can demonstrate all the skills and techniques in this book and carry them out safely, without relying on your instructor for advice. You'll be ready for your test when you can show that you've reached the standards set in this book – not before.

Don't come for your test before you're ready. Many people fail their test because they haven't had enough practice and experience – don't be one of them.

Remember, the learners who pass first time do so because they

- are well instructed
- get plenty of practice
- wait until they're ready.

Study materials

It's strongly recommended that you study *The Official Highway Code*. This is essential reading for all drivers. It contains the most up-to-date advice on road safety and the laws that apply to all road users. You can buy a copy from most booksellers and it's also available on CD-ROM, as an eBook and as an iPhone app.

Know Your Traffic Signs contains most of the signs and road markings that you're likely to come across.

The DSA series of books will provide you with sound knowledge of driving skills and safe practices.

The Official DSA Guide to Driving – the essential skills is the official reference book, giving practical advice and best driving practice for all drivers.

You'll only need to pass a theory test if you want to drive vehicles other than those covered by this book.

The Official DSA Theory Test for Car Drivers includes all the revision questions and answers for the multiple choice part of the theory test and it explains why the answers are correct – lots of useful information.

The revision questions are updated from time to time; make sure that you have the latest version. If you're well prepared you won't find the questions difficult.

This information is also produced in DVD-ROM format and as an iPhone app for those who prefer an interactive way of learning. In these formats you can take as many mock tests as you like before you actually take your test.

The Official DSA Guide to Hazard Perception is an interactive DVD to help you prepare for the hazard perception part of the test.

It has clear guidance on how to recognise and respond to hazards and is packed with useful tips, quizzes and expert advice. It also includes interactive hazard perception clips and your performance will receive a score so you'll know if you're ready to pass.

These training materials are available online at **tsoshop.co.uk/dsa** or by mail order from **0870 600 5522**. They're also available from all good bookshops and selected computer software retailers.

The practical driving test

The driving test is straightforward. You'll pass if you can show your examiner that you can

- drive safely
- complete the set exercises
- demonstrate through your driving that you have a thorough knowledge of The Highway Code.

Your examiner wants you to do well and will try to put you at your ease.

How will the test be carried out?

This depends on the type of vehicle you use for the test.

When booking your test, make it clear which type of vehicle you'll be using.

Categories F, G, H, K These vehicles usually have only one seat, or they may have a passenger seat where the examiner would not be able to watch the driver. For these tests, the examiner will give you instructions at the side of the road and watch how you drive as you go around left and right circuits.

Very slow vehicles Such as pedestrian-controlled vehicles. Your examiner may walk along near you where he or she can watch your driving.

The test

The driving test is designed to see if you

- can drive safely
- know The Highway Code and can demonstrate this through your driving.

The test takes about 40 minutes.

Listen carefully to the examiner and if there's anything you don't understand, ask. Your examiner will realise that you may be nervous and won't mind explaining again.

Test routes Your examiner will use a test route that will

- include a range of typical road and traffic conditions
- take into account the size, weight and speed limitations of your vehicle.

Driving during the test Drive in the way that your instructor has taught you. If you make a mistake, don't worry; it might be minor and may not affect your result.

If during the test your examiner considers you to be a danger to other road users, your test will stop. Make sure that you're properly prepared and wait until you reach the standards set out in this book before you take your test again.

Does the standard of the test vary?

No. All examiners are trained to carry out the test to the same standard.

You would have the same result from different examiners or in different areas.

Are the examiners supervised?

Yes, they're closely supervised. A senior officer may accompany your examiner during the test.

Don't worry about this. The senior officer won't be examining you, but making sure the examiner is testing you properly. The senior officer won't interfere with the test, so just carry on as if they weren't there.

Can anyone accompany me on the test?

Yes, your instructor is allowed to be present during the test, but can't interfere or give you any help.

You should bring an interpreter with you if you need one. This can be your instructor if you wish.

Your interpreter must be at least 16 years old. If you want to bring an interpreter, please make this known when you book your test.

What will the test include?

All practical driving tests for specialist vehicles include

- an eyesight test (if you fail this, your test can't continue)
- an emergency stop
- Highway Code questions and road signs.

If you take your test on a vehicle in categories F or G (fitted with a reverse gear), you'll be asked to carry out at least one of these special exercises

- reversing round a corner
- turning in the road
- reverse parking.

Category H driving tests require you to drive the vehicle backwards and to turn your vehicle round, using its tracks, to face in the opposite direction. Your examiner will explain how you should perform this manoeuvre.

Category K driving tests don't include a reversing section.

The special exercises will take place at carefully selected places on the test route. Your examiner will be as helpful as possible, and for each exercise will

- ask you to pull up on the left at the side of the road
- explain the exercise and ask you to carry it out.

Booking your test

The easiest way to book your practical test is online or by telephone. If you book by these methods, you'll be given the date and time of your test immediately.

Online You can book online at **www.gov.uk** For Northern Ireland, use **dvani.gov.uk**

Telephone To book by telephone, call **0300 200 1122** (or **0845 402 4000** for bookings in NI). If you're deaf and use a minicom machine, call **0300 200 1144**. (For a minicom facility in NI ring **028 7034 1380**.) If you're a Welsh speaker, call **0300 200 1133**.

You'll need to know what category of vehicle test you want to book and provide

- your driver number, which is shown on your licence
- your driving school code number (if you have it)
- your credit or debit card details. Please note that the person who books the test must be the card holder. MasterCard, Visa, Delta and Visa Electron are accepted.

You'll be given a booking number and sent an appointment letter within a few days.

Post To book a practical test by post you'll need an application form. Application forms are available to download from **www.gov.uk** or on request from the DSA booking line. Send the form, together with the correct fee, to the address shown on the back of the form. Don't forget to give your preferred date when you book. Please

indicate on the form if you wish to take your test in Wales using the Welsh language. You may pay by cheque, postal order or with a credit/debit card. Please don't send cash. You'll receive an appointment letter within 10 days. Your confirmation will be sent in the post if you don't have an email address. Apply only when you're ready and well before the date you want to be tested.

Changing or cancelling your test
You can cancel or postpone your test online by visiting **www.gov.uk** or by telephone. You should contact the booking office at least three clear working days before your test date, otherwise you'll lose your fee. Only in exceptional circumstances, such as documented ill-health or family bereavement, can this rule be waived.

Home tests

As the vehicles in categories F, G, H and K are often limited as to how far they can travel, it's possible for your examiner to come to you. The booking office will send an acknowledgement of receipt of your application and ask you to suggest a suitable meeting place.

Your test has to take place on roads with traffic and junctions, so very remote locations may be unsuitable. Your examiner may need to telephone you to confirm the meeting place.

Attending your practical test

Documents

When you arrive for your test you need to have with you

- your provisional driving licence – if you have a photocard licence you must bring both parts with you
- your passport, if your licence doesn't show your photograph (your passport doesn't have to be British). No other form of identification is acceptable.

Any of the following licences are acceptable

- a provisional driving licence issued in Great Britain or Northern Ireland, or a full GB or NI licence giving the provisional entitlement
- an EC/EEA licence accompanied by a GB licence counterpart, if you want to take a test for a category not covered by your full EU licence.

If you have a full driving licence which was issued in another country but isn't eligible for exchange for a GB licence, you must have a GB provisional licence.

All documents must be original – DSA can't accept photocopies.

If you don't bring these documents on the day you won't be able to take your test and you'll lose your fee.

Your test vehicle

Make sure that the vehicle you intend to drive during the test is

- legally roadworthy and has a current MOT certificate if required
- fully covered by insurance for use on test and for you to drive.

Your examiner will ask you to sign a declaration that your insurance is in order. The test won't be conducted if you can't do so.

Your vehicle should also display

- a valid tax disc
- red L plates displayed to the front and rear (in Wales, you can use D plates).

Red L plates should **not** be displayed

- on any windscreen or back window where they could obstruct your view
- where they'll cover lights or indicators.

If you overlook any of these, your test may be cancelled and you could lose your fee.

The condition of your vehicle Your vehicle **MUST** be mechanically sound. All equipment required by law **MUST** be fitted and working correctly.

In addition, your vehicle **MUST**

- have clean, functional lights
- have clean number plates, suitably fitted*
- not be carrying a load, or be partly loaded
- not be towing a trailer
- not drop mud or any debris on the road.

*The rules governing the display of number plates for vehicles covered by this book are contained in The Road Vehicles (Display of Registration Marks) Regulations. This can be found online at **legislation.gov.uk**

Unsuitable vehicles Your examiner will also check that your vehicle is suitable for use on a practical driving test. The test can't be conducted if the vehicle

- is operating on trade number plates
- doesn't display a valid tax disc

- is carrying any loose items that could fall off
- has damaged lights or indicators
- has broken or missing mirrors
- is carrying any load
- could be a danger to other road users due to damage
- is fitted with an item of equipment that may cause a danger to other road users
- has such a poor view that you need another person to help when carrying out manoeuvres or at junctions (the driver must be able to see well enough to drive safely during the test without needing assistance from anyone else).

section **two**
THE DRIVING TEST

This section covers
- The eyesight test
- Safety checks
- Before you start the engine
- The vehicle controls
- Other controls
- Moving off
- Rear observation
- Giving signals
- Acting on signs and signals
- Making progress and controlling your speed
- The emergency stop
- Reversing round a corner
- Reverse parking
- Turning in the road
- Hazards
- Selecting a safe place to stop
- The Highway Code questions and road signs

The eyesight test

What the test requires

You must satisfy your examiner that, in good daylight, you can read a vehicle number plate with letters of a certain size from a specified distance. If you need glasses or contact lenses to read the number plate you'll have to wear them throughout the test and whenever you drive.

F, G, H

You'll have to read a number plate with letters 79.4 mm (3.1 inches) high at a minimum distance of 20.5 metres (about 67 feet). Number plates with a narrower font should be read from a distance of 20 metres (about 66 feet).

K

You'll have to read the number plate at a minimum distance of 12.5 metres (about 41 feet).

How your examiner will test you

Before you start driving, your examiner will point out a vehicle and ask you to read its number plate. If you can't speak English, or have difficulty reading, you may copy down what you see. If your answer is incorrect, your examiner will measure the exact distance and repeat the test.

If you fail the eyesight test

If you can't show your examiner that your eyesight is up to the required standard

- you'll have failed your driving test
- your test will go no further
- you shouldn't drive again until you've had your eyesight corrected.

> **Remember,** if you normally wear glasses or contact lenses, always wear them whenever you drive or ride.

Age identifier

Local memory tag

Local memory tag

Safety checks

What the test requires

You must satisfy the examiner that you're capable of preparing to drive safely by carrying out simple safety checks on the vehicle you're using on the test.

You'll be expected to know how to carry out checks on any of the following, if they're appropriate to your vehicle

- tyres
- brakes
- fluids
- lights
- reflectors
- direction indicators
- horn.

How your examiner will test you

At the start of the test, the examiner will ask you one question

- to explain how you would carry out certain safety checks
- to demonstrate how you would carry out certain safety checks.

What your examiner wants to see

The examiner wants to see

- that you're familiar with the vehicle you're using for the test

- that you can explain, and in some cases demonstrate, how you would carry out simple safety checks on the vehicle you're using on the test.

If they're appropriate to your vehicle, the examiner could ask you about checking

- tyres for correct pressure and condition

- brakes (including the parking brake) for working order before any journey

- fluid levels (including screenwash, brake fluid, engine oil and coolant) – where they are and how you would check the levels

- reflectors and lights (including brake lights and direction indicators) for good working order and visibility

- other components (including steering, horn and warning devices) for good working order.

Information about these safety checks can be found in the basic maintenance section of *The Official DSA Guide to Driving – the essential skills* or in the vehicle handbook.

Faults to avoid

Being unable to explain or demonstrate basic safety checks on the vehicle you're using for the test.

Questions

The questions asked will depend on the category of vehicle used for the test. For example, the examiner might ask you to identify where the windscreen washer reservoir is and to tell them how you'd check the windscreen washer level.

If you give the wrong answer for one or both questions, you'll be marked with one driving fault.

Before you start the engine

What the test requires

You need to make sure it's safe to start and drive your vehicle. Your examiner will watch to see that you check and adjust your seat and mirrors (if you have them), that you make sure it's safe to start the engine and that you follow the correct procedures.

You need to check that

- you can reach and operate the main driving controls
- the brakes are applied
- the drive or gear selector is in neutral
- the hand throttle, accelerator or engine starting controls are properly set.

Skills and procedures

All vehicles

- Adjust the seat.
- Adjust the mirrors.
- Check that the gear lever is in neutral.
- Start the engine.

 F

Make sure the cab doors are closed.

As well as adjusting the position of the seat, you may have to make an adjustment for your weight.

Check that the hand throttle is set correctly, if you have one.

 G

If your vehicle has a fuel tap, make sure it's turned on.

Set the hand throttle. If you're driving a steam roller this doesn't apply, since you probably fired up an hour or two previously.

H

Adjust your seat. You should sit so that you're high enough to see directly. On military-style vehicles this means without looking through vision blocks.

Check your mirrors and adjust, if necessary. It's important to get them right, since later adjustment may not be possible.

If your vehicle has a fuel tap, make sure it's turned on.

Make sure the brakes are fully applied and latched.

K

For a mowing machine, the blades should be disengaged and in the travelling position.

Faults to avoid

- Starting in gear.
- Making the engine race.
- Keeping the starter motor engaged longer than necessary.
- Having to stop and readjust your seat.
- Adjusting your mirrors on the move because you didn't adjust them properly to start with.

The vehicle controls

The controls

Unlike cars, the controls of the vehicles covered by this book aren't standardised, so it's important that you study and learn the layout of your vehicle thoroughly.

The advice given in this book may not apply exactly to your vehicle. Make sure you understand the differences and how they affect you.

What the test requires

You should show your examiner that you understand the functions of all the controls. You should use them

- smoothly
- correctly
- safely
- at the right time.

The main controls are

- accelerator or throttle
- clutch, if not automatic transmission
- footbrake or main brake
- parking brake (handbrake)
- steering
- gears.

You should

- understand what these controls do
- be able to use them competently.

Skills and procedures

All vehicles

Accelerator and clutch Balance the accelerator and clutch to pull away smoothly.

- Accelerate smoothly to gain speed.
- When stopping, disengage the clutch just before you stop.
- Use the accelerator smoothly at all times.

Footbrake Brake smoothly and in good time.

Parking brake Know how and when to apply the parking brake.

Gears Choose the right gear for your speed and the road conditions.

- Change gear in good time.
- If you're driving an automatic vehicle, make sure the brakes are applied when you first engage 'drive' ('D').

Steering Keep your steering movements smooth and steady.

- When turning a corner, turn accurately and at the correct time.
- Steer a steady course.

F

Accelerator Use a foot-operated accelerator instead of a hand throttle or 'cruise control' for on-road driving. Hand throttles are normally for off-road work.

Footbrake If your tractor has a split left and right braking system, use the pedals locked together. Even when you're doing this, your tractor may 'pull' to one side or the other slightly, especially if you've been working off-road using the independent brakes.

Gears Make sure you're in the right gear range and using two-wheel drive.

Steering Keep both hands on the steering wheel unless you're operating another control.

G

Road rollers have a variety of controls, from a conventional car-style system to a hydraulic drive system. A hand throttle sets the engine speed, and transmission is controlled by a forward/reverse lever, with the brake being applied in the central neutral position.

Accelerator or hand throttle Set the hand throttle to the correct level without the engine racing.

Brake Brake smoothly and in good time. A heavy vehicle with steel rollers can be difficult to stop quickly.

Parking brake Know how and when to apply the parking brake. If the brakes operate as part of the forward and reverse control, it may have a lock to keep it secured.

Gears Choose the right gear for your speed and the road conditions. Plan your gear changes well in advance and try not to lose speed as you change.

If you're driving an automatic vehicle, make sure the brakes are applied when you first engage 'drive' ('D').

Steering Keep both hands on the wheel whenever possible, even if you have a steering ball.

Control of track-laying vehicles has almost become standardised to a 'two-stick' system of steering and braking. Occasionally you may come across a vehicle controlled by a steering wheel. If you have to drive that type of vehicle, make sure you understand its controls thoroughly. Transmission is normally of the semi-automatic or fully manual gearbox type, often with high/low ranges.

Make sure that you're not using the accelerator against the brakes when trying to stop in a straight line.

Clutch When stopping, don't disengage the clutch until just before you stop. This allows the engine braking to help you stop smoothly and in a straight line.

Accelerator Use the accelerator smoothly at all times but especially when changing gear. You need to coordinate gear changes with the accelerator even with semi-automatic gearboxes.

Brakes Apply the brakes evenly. Brake smoothly and progressively. Harsh braking can make the tracks slide, especially on wet roads. As these vehicles are steered via the braking system, you should be prepared for uneven braking.

Brake latches Know how and when to apply the brake latches, and also how to release them.

Gears Choose the right gear and range for your speed and the road conditions.

If you're driving a semi-automatic vehicle, make sure the brakes are applied when you first engage a gear.

Steering Keep both hands on the steering controls except when operating other controls.

On a road with a camber, tracked vehicles will wander down the slope without repeated correcting. Try to make frequent small corrections rather than occasional large ones.

When you're turning, the back of your vehicle will normally swing in the opposite direction. Allow for this when you turn.

K

These vehicles may have

- automatic transmission
- two-speed transmission
- a hydraulic drive controlled by a forward/reverse lever or pedal.

Accelerator or hand throttle If you have a hand throttle, don't let the engine race.

Clutch The clutch should be used smoothly. If releasing the clutch applies the brakes, remember that releasing the brake will also engage the clutch.

Footbrake Brake smoothly and in good time.

Parking brake Know how and when to apply the parking brake. Vehicles with automatic or hydraulic drive systems can creep forward when not held securely in place.

Gears Choose the right gear or ratio for your speed and the road conditions.

When going from forward to reverse (or reverse to forward, of course), bring your vehicle to a complete stop before engaging the opposite gear.

Steering Use both hands at all times, except when operating other controls. Steering balls should be used off-road only.

The back of rear-wheel-steered vehicles will swing the opposite way when you turn. You must allow for this.

Faults to avoid

Accelerator or hand throttle

- Accelerating fiercely, especially making the tyres screech or spin. This can lead to a loss of control and may distract or alarm other road users, including pedestrians.
- Making the vehicle surge or lurch by using the accelerator or hand throttle harshly.

Clutch Harsh use of the clutch when moving off or changing gear.

Footbrake Braking harshly, except in an emergency.

Parking brake

- Applying the parking brake before the vehicle has stopped moving.
- Moving off with the parking brake on.
- On a vehicle fitted with automatic transmission, failing to set the parking brake when waiting in queues or at junctions and allowing the vehicle to creep forwards.

Gears

- Taking your eyes off the road to look at the gear lever.
- 'Coasting' with the clutch disengaged or the gear lever in neutral.

Steering Don't turn too early when steering around a corner. If you do, you risk

- cutting the corner when turning right and putting other drivers at risk
- striking the kerb when turning left.

Don't turn too late. You could put other road users and pedestrians at risk by

- swinging wide on left turns
- overshooting on right turns.

Don't weave when travelling a steady course. If you do, you risk

- alarming oncoming drivers
- putting other road users in danger.

Other controls

What the test requires

You should understand the functions of all controls and switches that have a bearing on road safety, including

- lights
- indicators
- windscreen wipers
- demister
- heater.

You should know where to find these controls on the vehicle you're driving and be able to use them without taking your eyes off the road. If you need to use these controls but can't – either because of conditions during the test, or because you don't know how – you may fail your test.

You need to know the meaning of any gauges or warning lights, and be able to read the speedometer accurately.

Safety checks

You should be able to carry out routine checks on

- oil and coolant levels
- tyre pressures
- hydraulic fluid levels.

You should also be able to identify faults with

- steering
- brakes
- tyres
- lights
- reflectors
- horn
- rear-view mirrors
- speedometer
- exhaust system
- direction indicators
- windscreen wipers and washers.

Moving off

What the test requires

During the test you'll have to move off from the side of the road several times. You may have to move off on a slope and from behind a parked vehicle.

How your examiner will test you

Your examiner will watch carefully to make sure that you carry this out safely and without obstructing other road users.

In particular, you must ensure that

- you check to make sure it's safe
- you signal, if it would help another road user or pedestrian
- you use the controls smoothly and safely
- you don't make other road users change speed or direction to avoid you.

Skills and procedures

All vehicles

- Select the correct gear.
- Check your mirrors and look all round.
- Signal if necessary.
- If safe, move off smoothly, coordinating accelerator and clutch.

F

An engine cover could block your view of a child just in front of you.

Modern tractor cabs have slim frames, but these can still cause blind spots.

G

Look all round. Pay particular attention to any areas you can't see easily because of the construction or size of your vehicle. Even an exhaust could cause a blind spot large enough to hide a pedestrian.

H

You often have a very limited view in a category H vehicle, so make good use of your mirrors. You could even stand up and have a look round if in doubt.

As you move off don't turn too sharply, as the back of your vehicle may swing to the left, hitting the kerb. This could damage the kerb and/or your tracks and endanger pedestrians. There's also the possibility that the tracks could jump off the guide wheels, resulting in a serious loss of control and damage to your vehicle.

> **Remember,** vehicles in categories F, G, H and K may have noisy engines, so you may not be able to hear approaching vehicles.

K

This type of vehicle is unlikely to have mirrors, so look all round.

If you have rear-wheel steering, don't turn too sharply or your wheels could hit or mount the kerb, endangering pedestrians.

Faults to avoid

- Moving off into the path of another road user.
- Stalling.
- Using the wrong gear.
- Rolling backwards on an uphill slope.
- Lurching or jerking.
- Causing another road user to change speed or direction.

Rear observation

What the test requires

During the test your examiner will be watching to see that you use your mirrors at the correct time, and act properly on what you see. There may be times when you need to look behind, as well as using your mirrors. For vehicles without mirrors you need to turn and look behind instead.

Make sure that you use your mirrors or look behind effectively

- before any manoeuvre
- so that you're always aware of what's happening behind you.

Check carefully before

- moving off
- signalling
- changing direction or position
- passing parked cars or obstructions
- turning to the left or right
- overtaking or changing lanes
- increasing speed
- slowing down or stopping.

If your vehicle has a driver's door opening onto the road, you must check that the area is safe before opening it.

You should be aware that mirrors won't show everything behind you.

Skills and procedures

All vehicles

- Always check your mirrors before signalling. Use the Mirrors – Signal – Manoeuvre (MSM) routine (see page 54). If you don't have mirrors, turn and look instead.
- Check your mirrors frequently.
- Act safely and sensibly on what you see.
- Mirrors may not show everything – turn and look when necessary.

F, G

Where fitted, the mirrors on these vehicles can be affected by severe vibration. If your vehicle is affected, you'll have to turn and look behind.

H

Track-laying vehicles may have a poor rear view, which means you must rely on the mirrors. They must be properly adjusted and clean.

Always check your mirrors before signalling. Use the MSM routine.

Keep checking your mirrors frequently. You need to notice if a vehicle behind you disappears – possibly into a blind spot.

Act safely and sensibly on what you see.

These machines aren't normally fitted with mirrors, therefore you need to turn and look behind.

Look behind you frequently and act safely and sensibly on what you see.

Faults to avoid

* Signalling or changing speed or direction without checking behind first.

* Not acting correctly on what you see.
* Spending so much time looking in your mirrors that you miss things ahead.

Use of mirrors and rear observation

Rear observation means a combination of mirror checks and looking behind to ensure you're always fully aware of what's happening behind you.

Looking behind is important when the view through the mirrors is restricted or blurred.

Use judgement in deciding when to look behind. When you're looking behind you're not looking ahead, which could be hazardous in some situations. Equally, there are situations when it's dangerous not to look behind; for example, before moving off.

Giving signals

During your test you'll have to give signals to let other road users know what you're going to do.

You should signal

- to let others know what you intend to do
- to help other road users, including pedestrians
- in plenty of time.

Your examiner will watch to make sure that you signal clearly, without confusing other road users. You must only use the signals shown in The Highway Code.

Your signals should help other road users to

- understand what you intend to do
- react safely.

Always make sure that your signal is cancelled after use.

Even if your vehicle has indicators and brake lights, you should still know how to give arm signals and when they may be necessary.

All vehicles

Always check your mirrors before signalling. (Use the MSM routine.)

Give signals clearly and in good time. When using indicators, make sure you cancel them after use.

F, G, K

When your vehicle is travelling slowly, early signals help other road users react in good time. However, giving signals too early could mislead other road users.

If your vehicle doesn't have indicators, you'll have to use arm signals. Use only the signals shown in The Highway Code.

If you give arm signals, you may have to repeat them several times.

H

Make sure you cancel your indicators after use. Repeater warnings may not be easy for you to see or hear.

It's unlikely you'll be able to give arm signals when driving this type of vehicle.

Faults to avoid

- Giving signals carelessly.
- Misleading other road users.
- Forgetting to cancel the signal.
- Waving at pedestrians to cross the road.

41

Acting on signs and signals

What the test requires

You must be able to understand

- all traffic signs and signals
- all road markings.

You must react to them in good time.

How your examiner will test you

Your examiner will watch carefully how you react to signals and road markings. You'll be asked to turn at junctions. Make sure you act on all lane markings and direction signs.

Your examiner won't tell you about normal road signs. You must see them and act on them correctly.

Signals by other road users Watch for signals from other road users and

- react correctly and in good time
- don't rely on another road user's signal; it may have been left on by accident
- be careful how you react to signals not given in The Highway Code. The person giving the signal might not mean what you think they mean.

Traffic lights You **MUST** act correctly at traffic lights.

- Make sure the road is clear before proceeding at green traffic lights.
- React promptly and safely at amber traffic lights.
- Stop in the right place at red traffic lights.
- Watch for filter lights and react safely to them.

Signals given by authorised persons
You **MUST** obey the signals given by

- police and traffic officers
- traffic wardens
- school crossing patrols.

Traffic-calming measures Take extra care on roads which have been altered by the addition of

- 20 mph (32 km/h) speed limit zones
- speed restriction humps
- width restrictions marked by bollards, posts or paved areas.

Skills and procedures

React correctly and in good time to all signals, signs and road markings. Watch for height, width or weight restrictions that could affect you and comply with them.

Faults to avoid

- Blocking junctions, even if not marked with a yellow box or 'keep clear' markings.
- Reacting late to signals or road markings.
- Reacting incorrectly to someone else's signal.

Making progress and controlling your speed

What the test requires

You should make reasonable progress along the road, bearing in mind

- road conditions
- traffic
- weather
- road signs and speed limits
- the capabilities of your vehicle.

Avoid driving unnecessarily slowly.

If you're driving a slow-moving vehicle, be prepared to pull over in a safe place and allow vehicles behind you to pass.

How your examiner will test you

Your examiner will be watching to make sure you control the speed of your vehicle correctly, adjusting your speed to suit the conditions at the time.

You should

- take care in the use of speed
- make sure that you can stop safely, well within the distance that you can see is clear
- leave a safe distance between yourself and other vehicles
- leave extra distance on wet or slippery roads

- approach junctions and hazards at the correct speed
- make progress while keeping within
  - speed limits
  - your vehicle's limitations
  - your limitations
- show sound judgement when emerging from junctions.

Skills and procedures

Drive at a speed appropriate to the road and traffic conditions, so that you can

- stop within the distance you can see to be clear
- react to any sudden changes in the road surface.

Faults to avoid

- Driving too fast or too slowly for the road and traffic conditions.
- Breaking speed limits.
- Changing your speed unpredictably.
- Leaving your braking until the last possible moment.
- Using a hand throttle unnecessarily when a foot accelerator is available. If you have to use a hand throttle, make sure it's shut down when the vehicle is stationary.

The emergency stop

What the test requires

Whenever you drive, there's the possibility that something will cause you to brake suddenly. You'll need to react quickly and correctly in such situations.

As part of your tractor or specialist vehicle driving test, you have to show your examiner that you can stop your vehicle correctly in such an emergency.

You should be able to stop

- as quickly as possible
- safely
- under control.

How your examiner will test you

Your examiner will

- ask you to pull up at the side of the road
- ask you to stop as in an emergency when you're given the signal
- demonstrate that signal to you.

Your examiner will check that the road is clear behind you before the signal is given and will be watching carefully to see that you can stop

- in a short distance
- under full control
- without risk to other road users.

When your examiner gives the signal you should try to stop as you would in a real emergency. You should

- react quickly
- stop in a straight line
- take account of the road conditions.

Skills and procedures

All vehicles

- React as quickly as possible.
- Brake firmly.
- Control your braking, so that you're stopping as quickly as possible without locking the wheels.
- Use both hands to control the steering.
- Just before the vehicle stops, disengage the clutch to keep the engine running.

F

The large, chunky tyres fitted to tractors can give limited grip on asphalt roads. Be prepared to take immediate corrective action if you overbrake and skid, especially on wet roads.

Tractors with a split left and right braking system can veer to one side even when the brake pedals are locked together. Be prepared for this and take immediate corrective action if this happens.

G

Although a road roller doesn't travel very fast, its weight can make it difficult to stop.

Metal rollers have little grip. Braking too hard for the road conditions can make even a road roller skid.

H

Tracked vehicles are usually stopped by applying the brakes to each track with a separate lever. You must make sure you apply the brakes evenly on each side.

If the brakes are applied unevenly, the vehicle will veer to one side. Harsh braking can

- tip the vehicle forward, leading to loss of control
- lead to skidding, since tracks don't grip asphalt very well.

K

Soft tyres designed for use on grass may not grip well on wet roads.

Pedestrian-controlled vehicles are usually

- slow
- light
- easy to stop.

However, harsh application of the brakes could still cause skidding, especially on wet roads.

Faults to avoid

- Anticipating the examiner's signal by slowing or stopping while your examiner is checking the road behind.
- Skidding out of control.
- Allowing the vehicle to swing off-course.

Reversing round a corner

What the test requires

Your examiner may ask you to reverse into a side road to demonstrate your ability to control the vehicle in reverse.

You should be able to reverse

- smoothly
- accurately
- safely
- under full control
- with due regard for the safety of other road users.

Note
You won't be asked to carry out this manoeuvre if you're using a vehicle in categories

- H
- K.

How your examiner will test you

Your examiner will normally

- ask you to pull up just before a side road on the left
- point out the side road and ask you to reverse into it, straighten up and continue to reverse for a reasonable distance.

If your view to the rear is restricted, your examiner might ask you to reverse into a road on the right.

Skills and procedures

All vehicles

- Look all round before moving off. The construction of your vehicle may cause blind areas which could hide pedestrians.
- Keep your speed down while reversing.
- Look for passing vehicles. The front of your vehicle will swing out as you turn in. Be prepared to stop if necessary.
- Continue reversing for about two vehicle lengths, keeping reasonably close to the kerb.
- Look behind you, except when checking for passing vehicles and pedestrians.

F

You may be asked to reverse into a side road without a kerb. Don't let the wheels go onto the grass.

Large tractor wheels smooth out small bumps, so you may not feel the kerb if you hit or mount it.

The front of a tractor can swing a long way out when reversing into a side road. Before turning, look all round for passing traffic and stop if necessary.

G

Road rollers can easily damage the kerb if you let them bump or ride over it.

The noise of your engine and rollers can mask the sound of other vehicles approaching. Keep looking all round.

- Mounting the kerb.
- Swinging out wide.
- Reversing too far from the kerb.
- Not showing consideration to other road users.
- Taking so long to complete the exercise that you create a hazard for other road users.
- Being too cautious.

Reverse parking

What the test requires

You should be able to park safely either at the kerb (by reversing into a space about twice the length of your vehicle) or off the road by reversing neatly into a parking bay.

How your examiner will test you

Parking at the kerb behind a parked vehicle After your examiner has explained what's required, you should

- drive alongside the parked vehicle and position your vehicle so that you can carry out the exercise correctly and safely
- select reverse gear – your reversing lights might help others to understand your intentions
- use effective all-round observation

- reverse into the space behind the parked vehicle and park within a distance of about twice the length of your vehicle
- stop reasonably close, and parallel, to the kerb.

Reversing into a parking bay You should

- look at the layout markings and the size of the space available
- use your mirrors and signal if necessary
- check your position and keep your speed down
- use effective all-round observation
- look out for pedestrians
- reverse and park as neatly as possible, with your wheels straight
- make sure that your vehicle is neatly parked between the layout markings in the bay.

Skills and procedures

All vehicles

You should

- reverse under full control, safely and steadily
- use good, effective all-round observation
- show consideration to other road users.

Note
You won't be asked to carry out this manoeuvre if you're using a vehicle in categories

- H
- K.

 F

Watch for the front of your tractor, since the height of your engine cover could make it difficult to judge your position. Look for pedestrians or cyclists who may be behind you as you reverse.

 G

When you're driving a large road roller, a high engine cover can make it difficult to judge your position.

When parking on the road, don't turn in too sharply or get too close to the kerb – if you hit or mount it your roller could easily cause damage.

Faults to avoid

You shouldn't

- get too close to a parked car or the layout markings
- mount the kerb
- swing from side to side
- park, at an angle, too far from the kerb or layout markings
- place too much reliance on interior/ exterior mirrors rather than taking good effective all-round observations
- be inconsiderate or cause a danger to other road users
- take more than a reasonable time to complete the exercise. This may cause an obstruction for other road users
- steer harshly while the vehicle is stationary ('dry' steering).

Turning in the road

What the test requires

You'll be asked to perform this manoeuvre. See page 53 for details of how your examiner will carry out tests on category H vehicles.

How your examiner will test you

Your examiner will

- indicate a suitable place and ask you to pull up
- ask you to turn your vehicle round in the road.

Skills and procedures

You should control your vehicle smoothly, making proper use of the

- accelerator
- clutch
- brakes
- steering.

Show awareness of other road users, including pedestrians. All-round observation is essential throughout the manoeuvre.

- Make sure that the road is clear in both directions.
- Drive forward, turning to the right as much as possible.
- Steer briskly to the left just before you pull up close to the opposite kerb.
- Check all round, especially your blind spots.

- Reverse, turning to the left as much as possible.
- Steer briskly to the right before you pull up close to the kerb behind you.
- Repeat if necessary until your vehicle is facing in the opposite direction, close to the kerb.

Keep a good lookout for other road users. Look to the rear before reversing and don't rely on mirrors while reversing.

Note
You won't be asked to carry out this manoeuvre if you're using a vehicle in category K.

F, G

The engine covers can make it difficult to judge your distance from the kerb. Being able to judge your position accurately is an important skill, which can take time to acquire. If a road roller just clips the kerb, it can seriously damage both the kerb and the roller.

Engine noise from these vehicles can drown the sound of other vehicles. Make sure you keep checking for passing traffic.

Faults to avoid

- Touching or mounting the kerb.
- Causing danger or not showing consideration to other road users.

- Causing an obstruction for other road users by taking an excessive length of time to complete the exercise.

H

How your examiner will test you

Your examiner will

- indicate a suitable place and ask you to pull up

- ask you to drive the vehicle backwards and to make it face in the opposite direction by means of its tracks.

To perform this manoeuvre you may be asked to

- reverse into an opening on either the right or left and complete the turn by pulling forward

- reverse across the road and complete the turn by means of the tracks

- reverse for a distance before using the tracks to turn to face the opposite direction.

When you first move off from the side of the road, don't turn too sharply. The back of your vehicle could swing into the kerb, risking damage to the kerb or your tracks.

Don't allow any part of your vehicle to overhang the pavement at any time during the manoeuvre.

When reversing you may have an extremely limited view to the rear. Go slowly, making good use of all your mirrors. If in doubt, you may even have to stop for a moment to check it's clear behind. Stand up and look if your view is poor.

Hazards – the correct routine

What the test requires

A hazard is any situation that could require you to adjust your speed or alter your course. You must take the correct action in good time to avoid danger.

How your examiner will test you

There's no specific manoeuvre for this aspect of the test. Your examiner will watch throughout the test to see how you deal with any hazards that you come across.

Look well ahead where there are

- road junctions or roundabouts
- parked vehicles or obstructions
- cyclists or horse riders
- pedestrian crossings.

Skills and procedures

You may have to deal with several hazards at once, or during a short space of time. By identifying the hazard early you'll have more time to take the correct action.

Mirrors – Signal – Manoeuvre routine Always use the MSM routine when approaching a hazard. For vehicles without mirrors, you'll have to turn and look behind instead. Use judgement when looking round, and don't spend so much time looking behind that you miss danger developing ahead.

M – Mirrors
Check the position of traffic around and behind you.

S – Signal
Signal your intention to change course or slow down. Signal in good time. Where appropriate use indicators, if your vehicle has them.

M – Manoeuvre
A manoeuvre is any change of speed or position, from slowing or stopping to turning off a busy road. This can be broken down into

- **P** – Position
- **S** – Speed
- **L** – Look.

P – Position Your vehicle must always be in the correct position for the manoeuvre. When a change of direction is required, move into position in good time.

Owing to the size of your vehicle there may be occasions when you have to straddle lane markings to avoid mounting the kerb or colliding with street furniture, such as lampposts or traffic signs, etc. When positioning, watch for other road users who may not understand the special requirements of your vehicle.

S – Speed Ensure that the vehicle is travelling at the correct speed to complete the manoeuvre.

L – Look Looking means three things

- **Assessing** – what you can see
- **Deciding** – depending on what you see
- **Acting** – either continue or wait.

Faults to avoid

- Causing other drivers to take evasive action to avoid your vehicle.
- Simply looking in the mirror isn't enough. You must act correctly on what you see.

Hazards – road junctions and roundabouts

What the test requires

You'll be expected to show the examiner that you know the correct actions to take when approaching junctions and roundabouts. You should

- use the MSM routine when you approach a junction or a roundabout
- position your vehicle correctly, adjust your speed and stop if necessary
- obey any road markings and use the correct lane. In a one-way street, choose the correct lane as soon as you can do so safely
- watch out for
  - motorcycles and cycles passing on your left
  - pedestrians crossing at or near junctions
- use effective observation before you enter or emerge from a junction.

How your examiner will test you

Your examiner will watch carefully and take account of your

- use of the MSM routine
- position and speed as you approach the hazard
- observation and judgement.

Skills and procedures

All vehicles

- Observe road signs and markings and act correctly on what you see.
- Use the MSM routine.
- Position your vehicle correctly.
- Control your speed correctly as you approach the hazard.
- Slow down in good time, without harsh braking.
- Judge the speed of the other traffic accurately before joining the new road.

F, G

These vehicles can take up a lot of room, especially where lanes are narrow. Make sure you position your vehicle accurately in your lane.

You may sit a long way from the front of your vehicle. At junctions you may need to creep slowly forwards, looking both ways until you can see it's safe to emerge.

Don't leave it too late before changing lanes to put yourself in the correct position.

You may have a limited view to the sides. Watch out for other vehicles coming up to the junction alongside you, especially cyclists and motorcyclists.

Give clear signals. If you have to give arm signals, you may have to repeat them several times.

Make sure you pick a gap large enough to allow you to emerge safely.

Roundabouts can cause problems for slow and small vehicles. A busy roundabout with fast-moving traffic can be dangerous if you can't keep up with other vehicles. You can follow the optional advice given in The Highway Code for cyclists and horse riders.

Keep to the left, treating each entrance and exit as a separate junction, crossing each stream of traffic when it's safe.

Faults to avoid

- Signalling incorrectly.
- Approaching the junction at the wrong speed.
- Positioning your vehicle incorrectly.
- Stopping or waiting unnecessarily.
- Entering a junction unsafely.

Hazards – overtaking

What the test requires

If you have to overtake any other road user you must do so safely, allowing enough room. Give motorcyclists, cyclists and horses at least as much room as a car. They might wobble, swerve or react unpredictably.

Allow enough space after overtaking and don't cut in.

Don't overtake

- if the road is narrow
- where your view is limited
- where signs or road markings prohibit overtaking
- if it would stretch the performance of your vehicle to its limits.

How your examiner will test you

Your examiner will watch and take into account your

- use of the MSM routine
- reaction to road and traffic conditions
- handling of the controls.

You should be able to judge the speed and position of vehicles

- you're planning to overtake
- that might be trying to overtake you
- coming towards you.

Overtake only when you can do so

- safely
- without causing other vehicles to slow down or alter course.

Skills and procedures

All vehicles

- Don't get too close to the vehicle ahead.
- Check that it's clear in front and behind.
- Signal.
- Give the other vehicle plenty of room.
- Check it's safe before moving back to the left.

F

If you overtake another vehicle while driving a tractor, make sure you leave plenty of room and don't try to squeeze past.

Ensure you have enough time to overtake and return to the left without cutting in.

G, K

It's unlikely that you'll need to overtake anything when driving a road roller or a pedestrian-controlled vehicle.

If you do need to move around parked vehicles, check behind before moving out and, if possible, allow enough room for a vehicle door to open. Don't move back to the left too soon.

Your vehicle may

* have very poor vision to the side and behind
* be much wider than normal.

This will make overtaking a difficult manoeuvre to perform safely. Before committing yourself to overtaking, make sure you have plenty of

* room
* time
* speed in reserve.

Faults to avoid

Overtaking when

* your view of the road ahead isn't clear
* you would have to break the speed limit.

Hazards – meeting and passing other vehicles

What the test requires

You should deal with oncoming traffic safely and confidently. This applies

- on narrow roads
- where there are parked cars or other obstructions on your side of the road
- where there's an obstruction on the right and oncoming traffic has moved over to your side of the road to get past.

Use the MSM routine, and be prepared to stop and give way. If you need to stop, keep well back from the obstruction to give yourself

- a better view of the road ahead
- room to move off easily when the road is clear.

When you're passing parked cars allow at least the width of a car door, if possible.

How your examiner will test you

Your examiner will watch carefully during the test and take into account your

- use of the MSM routine
- reaction to road and traffic conditions
- handling of the controls
- judgement and control when meeting oncoming traffic

- decision-making when moving off or stopping
- clearance when passing parked cars.

Watch out for

- doors opening
- children running out into the road
- pedestrians stepping out from between parked cars
- vehicles pulling out without warning.

Skills and procedures

All vehicles

- Look well ahead.
- Plan where to stop to allow other vehicles room to get past.
- When you pull into a gap, don't get too close to the parked cars.
- Look out for passing vehicles as you move off again.

F, G

Use the height of your vehicle to get a good look ahead. Don't try and squeeze through a tight gap. Misjudging your width could have serious consequences.

If you need to wait, don't get too close to the obstruction. Engine covers or bodywork may make it difficult to judge how much clearance you have.

H

Ensure you have a clear view of the situation. You must accurately judge your width and length.

Watch for the back of the vehicle swinging in the opposite direction as you steer.

K

Pedestrian-controlled vehicles

Remember to check for passing traffic before moving out around an obstruction.

K

Mowing machines

Be aware of the width of your cutters and shrouds when moving around and between parked cars.

For rear-wheel-steered vehicles, remember that the back of your vehicle has to move to the left for you to steer to the right, so don't get too close to parked vehicles.

Faults to avoid

- Stopping or waiting when it's safe and correct to proceed.
- Stopping where oncoming vehicles can't get past you.
- Passing through gaps too fast for safety.

Hazards – crossing the path of other vehicles

What the test requires

You should be able to cross the path of other vehicles safely and with confidence.

Crossing the path of other vehicles occurs when you have to turn right into a side road or driveway. You should show that you can turn right safely by using the MSM routine. You must correctly judge the speed of oncoming vehicles and choose the correct time to turn.

You should

- use the MSM routine
- position your vehicle correctly and adjust your speed
- keep as close to the centre of the road as is safe
- watch out for oncoming traffic and stop if necessary.

Watch out for pedestrians

- crossing the side road into which you intend to turn
- on the pavement if you're entering a driveway.

How your examiner will test you

The examiner will observe your driving and your judgement when turning right. You'll be expected to show confidence and sound judgement.

Don't cause other road users to slow down or change direction to avoid your vehicle.

Skills and procedures

All vehicles

- Use the MSM routine.
- Before turning right, position your vehicle just to the left of the centre of the road.
- Adjust your speed correctly.
- If you have to stop, do so in the correct place.
- Wait for a safe gap before turning.

With a tractor, good vision can make positioning and judgement of oncoming traffic easier. Take your acceleration rate into account when judging a safe opportunity to turn across approaching traffic.

Wait for a large enough gap in the oncoming traffic to allow for the slow acceleration of your vehicle.

As you may be waiting for longer than a car would, watch out for impatient drivers or riders trying to overtake as you turn.

As you start to turn, the back of your vehicle will swing to the left. This can be dangerous for traffic passing you on your left. Other drivers or riders may not know how your vehicle handles.

Faults to avoid

- Causing other vehicles to
  - slow down
  - swerve
  - stop.
- Turning too early and cutting the corner.
- Going too far forward before beginning to turn.

Hazards – following at a safe distance

What the test requires

Keep a safe distance between your vehicle and the vehicle in front. In good conditions this should be at least one metre for every mile per hour you're travelling, or a two-second gap. In poor conditions, this gap should be at least doubled.

In a queue of traffic, leave enough room to pull out around the vehicle in front in case it should break down.

How your examiner will test you

Your examiner will watch carefully and take account of your

- use of the MSM routine
- anticipation
- reaction to changing road and traffic conditions
- handling of the controls.

Skills and procedures

All vehicles

You should

- be able to judge a safe separation distance between your vehicle and the vehicle in front
- show correct use of the MSM routine, especially before reducing speed

- avoid the need to brake harshly if the vehicle in front slows down or stops.

Take extra care when your view ahead is limited by large vehicles, such as lorries or buses.

Watch out for

- brake lights ahead
- direction indicators
- vehicles ahead braking suddenly.

F

The height of a tractor can give you an excellent view of the road ahead, but longer braking distances mean you'll still have to leave plenty of room.

G

Unless you're in slow-moving traffic queues, you're not going to be close to the traffic ahead.

In a traffic queue, look well ahead and don't just react to the vehicle in front. Leave plenty of room, and try to brake in good time. Steel rollers can skid on wet roads if you brake hard and late.

The height of your vehicle helps by allowing you a good view of the road ahead.

H, K

In traffic queues keep a safe distance from the vehicle in front. This will allow you to pass it if it stops or breaks down.

Faults to avoid

- Following too closely.
- Braking suddenly.
- Stopping too close to the vehicle in front in a traffic queue.

Hazards – positioning and lane discipline

What the test requires

Correctly positioning your vehicle is an important part of driving. A badly positioned vehicle causes difficulties and confusion for other drivers. Normally, keep well to the left.

You should

- keep clear of parked vehicles
- avoid weaving in and out between parked vehicles
- position your vehicle correctly for the direction you intend to take.

You should obey all lane markings, especially

- left- or right-turn arrows at junctions
- when approaching roundabouts
- in one-way streets
- bus and cycle lanes.

How your examiner will test you

Throughout the test the examiner will observe your road position. You'll be expected to select the correct position in good time for all situations.

Skills and procedures

All vehicles

- Plan ahead and choose the correct lane in good time.
- Use the MSM routine correctly.
- Follow any road markings as soon as you can.
- Position your vehicle correctly, even if there are no road markings.

F, G

The height of these vehicles can make it easier to see and plan ahead. Road markings especially can be easier to see.

Get into your lane as soon as you can. The slower you're travelling, the harder it becomes to change lanes safely.

No matter how slowly you travel, bus and cycle lane restrictions will apply to you.

H

A wide vehicle can take up a whole lane. Try to keep to the middle of the lane, allowing other vehicles as much room as possible to get past.

K

Make yourself as visible as possible by wearing high-visibility clothing.

At busy roundabouts, pedestrian-controlled vehicles may find it safer to adopt the

procedure for cyclists in The Highway Code, rule 187.

Remember that bus and cycle lane restrictions will apply to you.

Faults to avoid

- Driving too close to the kerb.
- Driving too close to the centre of the road.
- Changing lanes at the last moment.
- Obstructing other road users by being badly positioned or being in the wrong lane.
- Straddling lanes or lane markings.
- Cutting across the path of other traffic at roundabouts.

Hazards – pedestrian crossings

What the test requires

Pedestrian crossings are safe only if drivers treat them correctly. The different types of pedestrian crossings are

- zebra crossings
- pelican crossings
- puffin crossings
- toucan crossings
- equestrian crossings.

At pelican, puffin, toucan and equestrian crossings you **MUST** stop if the lights are red.

- At a pelican crossing you should give way to any pedestrians on the crossing when the amber lights are flashing.
- At a toucan crossing you should give way to cyclists as you would to pedestrians
- At an equestrian crossing you should give way to horse riders as you would to pedestrians. Be careful not to rev your engine as this could frighten the horse.

How the examiner will test you

Your examiner will watch carefully and take account of how you deal with all types of pedestrian crossings.

You should be able to

- control your speed as you approach a pedestrian crossing

- stop safely if necessary
- move off when it's safe.

Skills and procedures

All vehicles

- On the approach to a pedestrian crossing, use the MSM routine.
- Approach so that you can stop easily if necessary.
- Before you move off, look for pedestrians hurrying onto the crossing.

F, G, H

Large, noisy vehicles can startle horses and be intimidating to pedestrians, especially children and older people. Approach with care. If you stop, wait patiently – the pedestrians may not react instantly.

K

Pedestrians may misjudge the speed of these vehicles. Be prepared for someone to step out at the last moment.

Faults to avoid

- Approaching a crossing too fast.
- Driving over a crossing without stopping or showing awareness of waiting pedestrians.
- Blocking a crossing by stopping directly or partly across it.

Don't hurry pedestrians by

- sounding the horn
- revving the engine
- edging forward.

Don't

- overtake within the zigzag white lines leading up to crossings
- wave pedestrians across the road
- react late or incorrectly to traffic light signals at controlled crossings.

Selecting a safe place to stop

What the test requires

Whatever vehicle you drive, you'll have to stop at the side of the road safely and without inconvenience to other road users. Normally, your examiner will leave it up to you where you stop. Occasionally you'll be asked to stop in a specific place. When stopping you should be able to select a place where you won't

- obstruct the road
- create a hazard
- break the law.

How your examiner will test you

Your examiner will watch and take account of your

- use of the MSM routine
- judgement in selecting a safe place to stop.

You should know how and where to stop without causing inconvenience or danger to other road users.

Skills and procedures

All vehicles

- Use the MSM routine.
- Select a safe place to stop.
- Brake and steer smoothly.
- Stop close to, and parallel with, the kerb.
- Normally stop with your wheels straight.

F, G

If you have a high cab, watch out for low tree branches or street furniture. If you hit or mount the kerb you may cause damage.

H

The rear of a tracked vehicle will swing towards the kerb as it moves off. Make allowance for this when you stop.

K

Mowing machines sometimes have cutter guards that increase the overall width. Don't allow these guards to overhang the pavement when you stop.

Faults to avoid

- Stopping without sufficient warning to other road users.
- Causing danger or inconvenience to other road users when you stop.
- Stopping anywhere The Highway Code says you shouldn't.

The Highway Code questions and road signs

What the test requires

You need to be familiar with the content of The Highway Code and your legal responsibilities as a road user.

How your examiner will test you

At the end of the test, you'll be asked five questions on The Highway Code and other motoring matters. You'll then be asked to identify six different traffic signs.

To prepare for these questions, study The Highway Code, which contains all the rules and a selection of the more common road signs and markings. This is available in

- book format
- electronic format
- as an app
- on DVD, accompanied by British Sign language.

In addition, *Know Your Traffic Signs* is a book that contains the vast majority of road signs you may encounter on the roads.

Skills and procedures

Be familiar with

- road signs and signals and what they mean
- various lines and markings on the road
- the rules, advice and legal issues relating to road use
- various other road user types, eg pedestrians, large vehicles, motorcyclists, etc.

Faults to avoid

Insufficient knowledge of the content of The Highway Code.

Inability to identify road signs, signals and markings.

section **three**
AFTER YOUR TEST

This section covers

- If you pass
- Developing your driving standards
- If you don't pass

If you pass

Well done. You've shown that you can drive safely and confidently. Your examiner will give you a copy of the driving test report showing any driving faults that were marked during the test, together with some explanatory notes.

Your examiner will then ask you for your provisional licence so that a full licence can automatically be sent to you through the post.

Your examiner will take your provisional licence and, once the details have been taken, will shred it. You'll be given a pass certificate as proof of success until you receive your new licence.

However, you don't have to surrender your licence if you don't want to, or in certain circumstances – for example, if you've changed your name.

In these cases you'll have to send your provisional licence, together with your pass certificate and the appropriate fee, to DVLA, who will then send you your full licence. You have to do this within two years or you'll have to take your test again.

In Northern Ireland, the examiner will issue you with a pass certificate and this, along with your licence, should be forwarded to DVA Licensing as soon as possible. No fee is required.

New Drivers Act

Your licence will be revoked if you receive six or more penalty points as a result of offences you commit within two years of passing your first practical test. This includes any offences you may have committed before passing your test.

If you get six penalty points, you'll have your licence revoked and you must then reapply for a provisional licence. You'll then have to drive as a learner until you pass the practical driving test again.

This applies even if you pay by fixed penalty.

Developing your driving standards

Passing your driving test is the first step to becoming a good driver. It means you've reached a safe basic standard.

You should aim to raise your standard of driving with additional instruction and experience.

The Official Highway Code

Keep a current copy of *The Official Highway Code* and refer to it often. It will keep you up to date with developments in driving rules and procedures. This is also available as an interactive CD-ROM, an iPhone app and in British Sign Language.

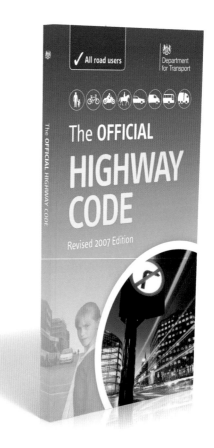

If you don't pass

Your driving isn't yet up to the required standard. You'll have made mistakes which have shown a lack of control or could cause danger on the road.

Your examiner will help by giving you

- a driving test report form. This shows all the faults marked during the test
- a brief explanation of why you haven't passed
- guidance notes.

Your examiner will be able to help you by pointing out the aspects of your driving that you need to improve.

Study the driving test report and refer to the relevant sections in this book. Show your copy of the report to your instructor, who should advise and help you to correct the faults. Listen to your instructor's advice carefully and get as much practice as you can.

Don't just practise the things for which you've failed; instead try to improve all aspects of your driving.

Right of appeal

You'll obviously be disappointed if you don't pass your driving test. Although your examiner's decision can't be changed, if you think your test wasn't carried out according to the regulations, you have the right to appeal.

If you live in England or Wales you have six months after the issue of the Statement of Failure in which to appeal (Magistrates' Courts Act 1952, Chapter 55, Part VII, Sect. 104).

If you live in Scotland you have 21 days in which to appeal (Sheriff Court, Scotland Act of Sederunt (Statutory Appeals) 1981).

If you live in Northern Ireland you can appeal to a Court of Summary Jurisdiction (Road Traffic Order 1981).

Before lodging an appeal you should seek legal advice.

section **four**

DRIVING LARGE, HEAVY OR SLOW VEHICLES

This section covers

- Planning your journey
- Amber beacons
- Dirty vehicles
- Carrying loads

Planning your journey

Route planning

When you've passed your test you may be driving large or slow vehicles on a variety of roads. Try and plan your route to avoid places where you could cause congestion and inconvenience to other road users.

Try to avoid

- busy roads
- known roadworks
- travelling during busy times of the day
- narrow roads with no passing places.

If you're causing a queue of traffic behind you, follow the advice in The Highway Code. Pull over where it's safe to do so and let traffic behind you pass.

Height, width and weight limits In order to drive safely on the road you need to know various details about your vehicle, particularly its

- height
- width
- weight
- length
- ground clearance.

Look out for all signs relating to these limits and make sure that you obey them.

Before you start your journey, plan your route and ask for advice if you don't know the area. Local authorities will know of any height, width and weight restrictions.

Motoring organisations may also be able to help if you're travelling further afield.

Low bridges The headroom under bridges in the UK is at least 5 metres (16 feet 6 inches), unless marked otherwise. (Lower bridges should be appropriately signed.) Where the overhead clearance is arched, this is normally only between the limits marked.

If your vehicle collides with a bridge, you **MUST** report the incident to the police. If a railway bridge is involved, report it to the railway authority as well by calling the number shown on the bridge identification plate or, if no plate is provided, call 999.

Do this immediately to avoid a possible serious incident or loss of life.

Give your name and telephone number, as well as information about

- the road name and bridge location
- the damage and when it occurred
- whether the vehicle is wedged under the bridge and if persons are trapped
- the vehicle registration number and owner's name
- your insurance details as the driver
- any bridge reference number (found on a plate bolted to the bridge or wall).

Electricity cables High-voltage electricity can 'jump' across a gap and overhead electricity lines are positioned to allow for a safe electrical distance.

Where overhead electricity lines cross public roads, there will normally be a clearance for vehicles of 5 metres (16 feet 6 inches) in height. At many agricultural or private crossings, the cables may be considerably lower. Warning signs and height gauges are provided and these must be complied with. The 'jump' gap clearance **MUST NOT** be compromised.

Take care if you are driving a high vehicle.

Level crossings You may need to call the railway controller at some railway level crossings if you're driving

- a long, low vehicle that may be at risk of grounding
- a large, slow vehicle that may take an abnormally long time to cross the railway line.

Signs will be displayed on the approach to the crossing and you **MUST** follow the instructions on the sign in these instances.

See Rules 291 to 299 in The Highway Code for information on negotiating various types of level crossing.

Motorways Motorways **MUST NOT** be used by

- holders of provisional ordinary licences
- pedestrians
- animals
- riders of motorcycles under 50 cc
- cyclists and horse riders
- agricultural vehicles
- certain slow-moving vehicles carrying oversized loads (except by special permission).

Amber beacons

On an unrestricted dual carriageway any vehicle with four or more wheels **MUST** display an amber beacon if it can't exceed 25 mph (40 km/h).

The beacon must be in a position where it can clearly be seen by other road users. If a trailer is being towed and this causes the beacon on the towing vehicle to be obscured, a beacon must be displayed on the rear of the trailer.

A beacon isn't required if the vehicle is only crossing the dual carriageway.

Dirty vehicles

Many of the vehicles covered by this book will be used in fields or on construction sites and roadworks. Before leaving the site you should check the vehicle to make sure it's safe and legal to take onto the road.

You should check that

- indicators and lights are clean
- number plates are clean and can be read easily
- windscreens and windows are clean
- the vehicle won't drop mud or any material on the road. Many sites have inspection and cleaning facilities near the exit. Make sure you use them.

Carrying loads

Any load that's carried on your vehicle or trailer **MUST** be secure. If you intend to carry a large load you should seek advice from the local police.

When loading any vehicle or trailer, the following points should be considered.

- Make sure the vehicle or trailer is capable of carrying the load.
- Keep any load beds clean and dry. This will help stop the load sliding.
- When carrying a small load, put it against the headboard.
- Always secure the load.
- If the bodywork of the vehicle or trailer is being used to contain the load, make sure it's strong enough to do so.
- Check there's no leakage.
- If you're using an open-backed vehicle or towing a trailer, use a sheet or a tarpaulin.
- Don't allow anything to blow off in the wind. Even dust from a vehicle can cause injuries to pedestrians.
- If you have to stack items, make sure the largest and heaviest ones are on the bottom.
- Make sure all anchorage points are secure and free of rust.
- Ensure any ropes you use are dry and in good condition.

- If the load has a large overhang either to the side or the rear, then you **MUST** put warning signs or lights on it.
- If the load covers the vehicle or trailer lights, then additional lights **MUST** be displayed.

Sharp edges

It's the driver's responsibility to make sure that the vehicle doesn't endanger other road users. There mustn't be any sharp edges or projections.

Agricultural implements, such as ploughs, have sharp edges. These must be protected and marked so that they're clearly visible to pedestrians.

Before being used on the road, mowing machines must have the blades stowed in the travelling position.

Index

Where can I find out more?

Driving Standards Agency

Whether you're learning to drive, helping others to learn or improving your skills, make sure you're using the official materials for expert information from the people who set the tests. For the full range of official DSA titles, go to tsoshop.co.uk/dsa

Did you know you can:

- book your theory test
- book your practical test

and much more by visiting www.gov.uk

or call customer services on 0300 200 1122

 Join the conversation

Questions about learning to drive? Follow **@Liz_DSA @John_DSA @Linda_DSA**

Keep up-to-date with the latest rules of the road **@HighwayCodeGB**

 Find out what to expect when you take your theory and practical driving tests:
youtube.com/dsagov

 mydrivingtest

Scan to become a fan for hints, tips and news for learners
(you'll need a phone with a QR code reader app to read the code)

HighwayCodeGB

Find out about all the latest rules of the road

Other official DSA publications

From the Driving Standards Agency -
the official route to Safe Driving for Life™

Driving Standards Agency

For learners

The Official DSA Theory Test for Car Drivers

Packed with official theory test revision questions and background information to help you really understand.

Book
ISBN 9780115532313   £14.99

Downloadable PDF*
ISBN 9780115532320   £14.99

DVD-ROM
ISBN 9780115531927   £12.99

Interactive Download*
ISBN 9780115531934   £9.99

The Official DSA Complete Theory Test Kit

Includes The Official DSA Theory Test for Car Drivers DVD-ROM and The Official DSA Guide to Hazard Perception DVD for complete theory test preparation.

DVD-ROM and DVD
ISBN 9780115531958   £19.99

* for instant access from tsoshop.co.uk

For all drivers

The Official DSA Guide to Hazard Perception

Develop your hazard perception skills and learn more about this part of the theory test.

DVD
ISBN 9780115528651   £15.99

The Official DSA Guide to Driving – the essential skills

Packed with advice for both learners and experienced drivers.

Book
ISBN 9780115531347   £12.99

Downloadable PDF*
ISBN 9780115531385   £12.99

eBook
Now available from your device's eBook store.

Rules of the road

Know Your Traffic Signs

Illustrates and explains the vast majority of traffic signs.

Book
ISBN 9780115528552   £4.99

The Official Highway Code

Essential reading for all road users.

Book
ISBN 9780115528149   £2.50

Interactive CD-ROM
ISBN 9780115528460   £9.99

British Sign Language Pack
ISBN 9780115529849   £9.99

eBook
Now available from your device's eBook store.

Official Highway Code iPhone app

All the rules of the road at your fingertips. Available on the iPhone app store.

 learningtodrive

 @DSA_Publishers

For the full range of official DSA titles and to place your order visit **tsoshop.co.uk/dsa** or call **0870 850 6553** quoting **CQD** when ordering. Also available from all good high street book stores.

information & publishing solutions

TSO (The Stationery Office) is proud to be DSA's official publishing partner. Prices and images are correct at time of going to press but may be subject to change without notice.